Making a Change for Good

Also by Cheri Huber

From Keep It Simple Books

The Key and the Name of the Key Is Willingness
That Which You Are Seeking Is Causing You to Seek
How You Do Anything Is How You Do Everything: A Workbook
There Is Nothing Wrong With You: Going Beyond Self-Hate
There Is Nothing Wrong With You for Teens
The Depression Book: Depression as an Opportunity for Spiritual Growth
The Fear Book: Facing Fear Once and for All
Nothing Happens Next: Responses to Questions about Meditation
Be the Person You Want to Find: Relationship and Self-Discovery
Sex and Money...are dirty, aren't they? A Guided Journal
Suffering Is Optional: Three Keys to Freedom and Joy
When You're Falling, Dive: Acceptance, Possibility and Freedom
Time-Out for Parents: A Guide to Compassionate Parenting
Trying to Be Human: Zen Talks
Good Life: A Zen Precepts Retreat with Cheri Huber
Buddha Facing the Wall
Sweet Zen: Dharma Talks with Cheri Huber
The Zen Monastery Cookbook: Stories and Recipes from a Zen Kitchen

From Hay House

How to Get from Where You Are to Where You Want to Be

Making a Change for Good

A Guide to Compassionate Self-Discipline

CHERI HUBER

SHAMBHALA
Boston and London
2007

Shambhala Publications, Inc.
Horticultural Hall
300 Massachusetts Avenue
Boston, Massachusetts 02115
www.shambhala.com

9 8 7 6 5 4

Printed in the United States of America

♾ This edition is printed on acid-free paper that meets the American National Standards Institute Z39.48 Standard.
♻ This book was printed on 30% postconsumer recycled paper.
For more information please visit us at www.shambhala.com.
Distributed in the United States by Random House, Inc.,
and in Canada by Random House of Canada Ltd

Designed by June Shiver

Library of Congress Cataloging-in-Publication Data
Huber, Cheri.
Making a change for good: a guide to compassionate self-discipline / Cheri Huber.—1st ed.
p. cm.
ISBN 978-1-59030-208-8 (alk. paper)
1. Self-control. 2. Control (Psychology) 3. Discipline. 4. Change (Psychology) 5. Conduct of life. I. Title.
BF632.H83 2007
170'44—dc22
2006050581

Contents

Making a Change for Good

1. Compassionate Self-Discipline and Presence: The Opportunity as We See It

I've never met anyone who does not struggle with self-discipline. The problem with self-discipline is usually identified as a lack of willpower, a lack of follow through. You commit to a program, with every good intention, and wake up a few days later having "failed."

A few of us are on the other side of the continuum, so disciplined we "fail" at things like kindness, spontaneity, and relaxation. One way or another, the struggle to be disciplined takes a lot of energy, often misspent.

There is a convoluted belief about self-discipline that many of us have taken on:

THE BELIEF

"If I were different - better, smarter, thinner, richer, more in control (which I would be if only I had more self-discipline!) - life would be as it should be and I would be happy. As it is, life isn't the way it should be and it's my fault!"

I contend that what we think of as the problem with self-discipline is not the problem at all, and the solutions we try, sincere as they are, lead only to frustration and failure. So, as I see it, this belief is not true.

Nothing in life is a matter of "fault";
no amount of self-discipline will ever give anyone control over life (control is an illusion);
happiness does not depend on circumstances;
and life is always exactly as it is!

There are two kinds of self-discipline.

1. Strict, harsh, and punishing

2. Supported, assisted, and nurtured

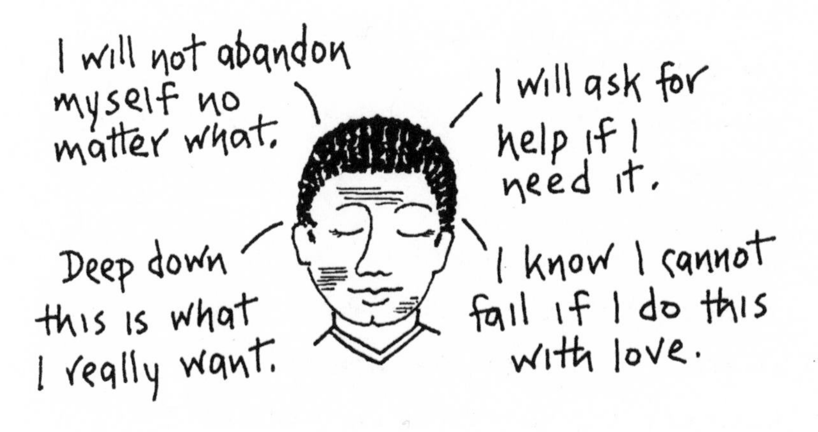

The first is familiar to us all.

The second, compassionate self-discipline, is nothing other than being present rather than engaged in distracted, unfocused, addictive behaviors based in an I-need-to-fix-myself mentality.

That person is actually paying attention, focusing on what is here to do in this moment, bringing compassion to all aspects of daily life, and discipline has nothing to do with it.

We don't lack self-discipline, we lack presence.

Compassionate self-discipline
is simply allowing
the intelligence and generosity
that is your authentic nature
to guide you in every moment.

With this guidance you will be not only disciplined, you will be spontaneous, clear, awake, aware, efficient, appropriate, respectful, grateful, kind, honest, sincere, expressive, steady, dependable, responsible, peaceful, joyful, and satisfied.

These are only a few descriptions of the experience.

Discovering compassionate self-discipline
may be easier and harder
than you thought.

On the one hand,
it is not necessary
to come up with more
sophisticated methods
for making your "self"
do what your self does not want to do.
No more planning, hoping, fearing, and failing.

On the other hand,
you will need to choose
in-the-moment presence
over the habitual patterns of a "conditioned mind."

CONDITIONED MIND

The everyday mind through which we interact with life is the result of a system of brainwashing called "socialization." From the first moment of life a child is taught what is right, wrong, ugly, beautiful, sacred, worldly, important, valuable, worthless; who the right people are, which values are important, which god to believe in, what heaven is, what hell is, how a person should be, how others should be, how the world should be, how people should be punished, what it means to be a man, what it means to be a woman...
In other words, every aspect of life has been programmed. (For most people, "going beyond" their childhood socialization is simply doing the opposite of what they were taught.) This program - whether adhering to it or rebelling against it - is what we call conditioned mind.

Everything you have attempted
for as long as
you can remember
has been under the direction
of a socially and karmically
conditioned mind.

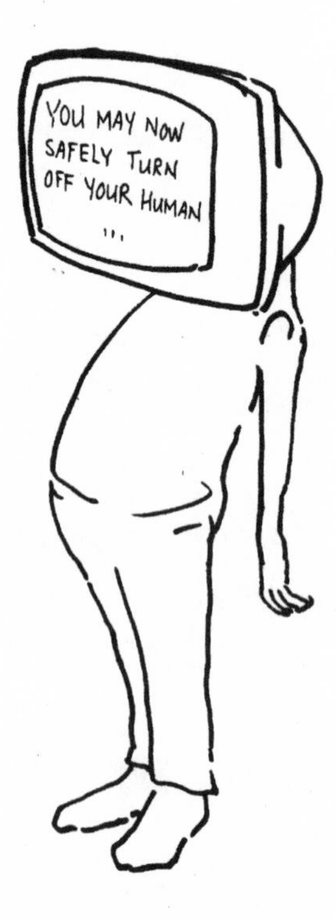

Every conditioned human being is in a constant, primary relationship with a voice in their head telling them, second by second, what is so, real, true, right, good, beautiful, worthwhile, important, and desirable, as well as what is wrong, bad, to be avoided, unpleasant, ugly, and so on.

The voice lets them know how they feel and if they're being the right person.

It scans for what's wrong and points out mistakes.

In other words, it creates and maintains the reality of each individual.

As you read this, the process I'm describing is going on. Conditioned mind is taking this in and looking to see if the information is true. Perhaps it's beginning to argue, "Do I agree with this? I don't have a voice in my head pointing out that stuff to me second by second."

That's it! That's the voice.

A casual observation will show you that you are constantly looking somewhere to get the information you're getting about every aspect of life. For instance, you decide to learn a new skill.

The decision, the approach, the beliefs about your abilities, success, failure, and so forth arise in conditioned mind. You may be aware of voices of enthusiasm or trepidation, and you may hear negative, even punishing voices saying you can't succeed because you have some built-in flaw that will prevent success. As you proceed, you are constantly following the directions, assumptions, and assessments coming from conditioned mind. You look to conditioned mind to tell you how you're doing. Depending on the response you get, you will feel good or bad. Are you learning this new skill quickly and easily? You get to feel good, proud, pleased. Are you learning it faster than others? Better still! Not meeting the standards? Oops. We know what that says about you.

Conditioned mind is framing your life,
and in this book we are going to
turn the tables on it.

Rather than "it" being in charge, calling the shots, making the decisions about what you do and how you feel, "you" will have the opportunity to observe "it" and to realize that you can have your own present-moment experience of life. You will have a chance to be in life without the filter of conditioning.

So the question is not
"How do I become more disciplined?"
The question is
"How do I learn to live in the present?"

EXERCISE

What does "self-discipline" mean to you?

What is your history with self-discipline?

What assumptions do you have about self-discipline?

2. Who's Talking?

Perhaps the greatest help in introspective work is sorting out "who the players are" - who is talking,

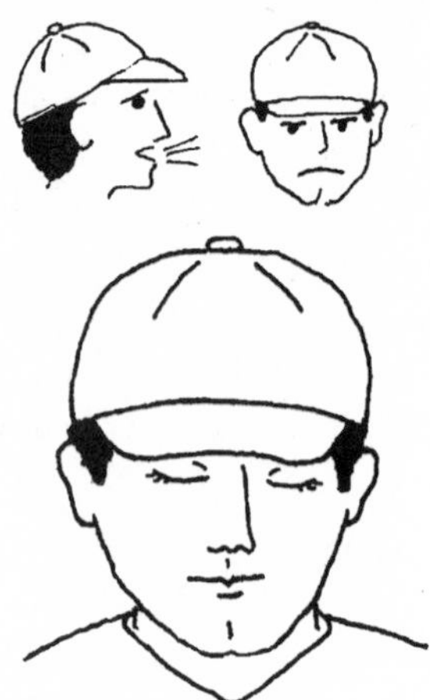

and who is listening.

The personality (the "I," "conditioned mind," who we think we are) is a composite of many parts, many aspects, many "subpersonalities." Subpersonalities are survival strategies we developed to make it through childhood. When you were being taught to fit into society - when you were being "socialized" - you concluded that you were the cause of other people's unhappiness, that there was something wrong with you, and that you needed to be different. You threw temper tantrums when you were two and three and they got you a lot of what you wanted. By the time you were four, that wasn't working anymore so you became a "performer" or a "helper," or you withdrew or rebelled, or you adapted in a way that, to your child's mind, seemed like it would be acceptable to those around you, get your needs met, and ensure your survival.

A new subpersonality was "born" each time you needed to adapt throughout your early years.

Now, as an adult, those parts of you are still operating. Sometimes you're talkative, other times withdrawn; sometimes you're charming, cautious, irritable, obsessed by a project, a procrastinator - the list is long for most people.

We learn to recognize subpersonalities by paying attention to what they say. They are many of "the voices in your head"; they are your "inner children." Each has a particular belief about whatever its area of interest is, and many are precisely opposite beliefs!

For me there is a student of Zen, a teacher, a writer, an athlete, a philosopher, an engineer, a psychologist, a mother, a daughter, a grandmother, a sister, a best friend, someone who is stubborn and tenacious, a soft-hearted marshmallow, an animal lover, a quick temper, crusader rabbit, champion of the underdog, and many more!

EXERCISE

Imagine going through an average day. "Who" wakes up in the morning? (Who picks out your sleepwear?) Who decides what to do first? Is someone in charge of the morning rituals? Who fixes breakfast? (Sometimes it might be the "health food fascist," sometimes the "junk food junkie.") Who decides what to wear? Is there someone who plans your day? A list-maker? A rehearser? Who goes to work (take a little time and consider that this might be a whole crew of subpersonalities, depending on circumstances)? Who plans your evening? Do you have a daydreamer, a fantasizer, a romantic, a veg-out-in-front-of-the-TV-with-beer-and-pizza? Who else?

Again, subpersonalities form to help us adjust to the ever-changing demands from those raising us. We were not acceptable as we were so we modified ourselves to get by. In my family it didn't work to be softhearted so I became mean and prickly to protect myself. Only after I found the safety of center was that soft-heartened person allowed to be a major player in my life.

CENTER

Center is the unconditionally accepting, conscious, compassionate awareness that is our authentic nature. It is the nonseparate reality that contains, and is able to embrace, the illusion of a separate self - called I, me, my - that suffers. When in center, everything is as it is and none of it is taken personally. There is nothing wrong; no loss, lack, or deprivation; no fear; no urgency. The feeling of center is often described as peaceful, compassionate, energetic, willing, and joyful. From center, the world is exactly the same as always, there's just nothing wrong.

In my experience, subpersonalities are feelings combined with beliefs and behaviors. The "responsible part of me" has beliefs about what being responsible is, acts the way it thinks it should, feels good or bad depending on meeting or not meeting standards, and projects like crazy on me and everyone else.

PROJECTION

When we look out at the world, we do not see the world as it is, we see the world as we are. The only thing we ever experience is ourselves. The world is simply a mirror. Simply put, if you are in a wonderful mood, if you've just fallen in love, the world is a glorious place full of beauty and promise. If you are miserable, if you just lost a pile of money in the stock market, the world is a hateful, hopeless, unfair place in which nothing good will ever happen for you. The world did not change.

Subpersonalities share a body with a bunch of other aspects, all calling themselves "I." As you attend closely, you can hear them talk back and forth...

about you!

Because aspects of the personality are there to meet specific needs, they are single-focused. The part that makes a commitment is not the same part that breaks it. They are two different subpersonalities. Each is there to take care of you in a particular way. Once a need is met, that subpersonality disappears and the next need arises, along with the aspect of the personality charged with meeting that need.

While subpersonalities may appear to be any age, emotionally they are rarely older than three or four years. They wreak havoc in our lives, demanding that we meet their needs (and all the "adult" versions of those desires), but children they are. Each was created to meet a need when we were too young to do anything but adapt and survive.

They aren't bad,
can't be gotten rid of,
and when embraced and appreciated
become delightful companions.

So, here you are with twenty or thirty small children who are depending on you for love, affection, guidance, structure, safety, and care. You don't get to decide which ones stay and which ones go, which ones live and which ones die! They're your CHILDREN!

They want stuff all the time,
like all good little children.
They're rambunctious,
frightened,
exuberant,
thoughtless,
adorable,
and utterly selfish.

They are meet-my-needs machines.
And, they're yours!
Lucky you.

I mean that "lucky you" part. Once you establish yourself as the conscious, compassionate presence who guides and cares for them, your fun quotient will go through the roof.

EXERCISE

List some of your subpersonalities and what they say. For example, which part of you says:

"I don't have time."

"I should have known better."

"I'll probably fail."

Add your own:

Perhaps there are things that happened when you were a child that you believe are beyond your ability to accept. That belief is conditioned mind at work again. It is sad, terribly sad, that awful things happen to children. There may never be a time when what happened to that child doesn't bring you to a place of deep sadness. There is nothing you can do about what happened then. And, you can do everything about now. You can comfort that child. You can embrace her in the unconditionally loving and accepting present. She may actually get to a place where she no longer feels sad. She may be so in the present that what happened in the past no longer matters to her. It is absolutely possible.

Conditioning often convinces us that embracing a suffering part of ourselves in compassion will be too painful, too horrible, and the child is abandoned to the suffering, left out of the present with no one there willing to make a difference. Conditioned mind will try to convince you it is too painful to face your suffering, and it will try to make you believe it is too painful to face the suffering in the world. Facing suffering, embracing suffering, becoming the conscious, compassionate awareness that can bring an end to suffering, is not painful. Trying to hide from suffering is extremely painful and will rob you of your life.

3. Meditation

Being present is what we practice in meditation - to be fully present to our experience, to see through the delusions of conditioned mind and end suffering.

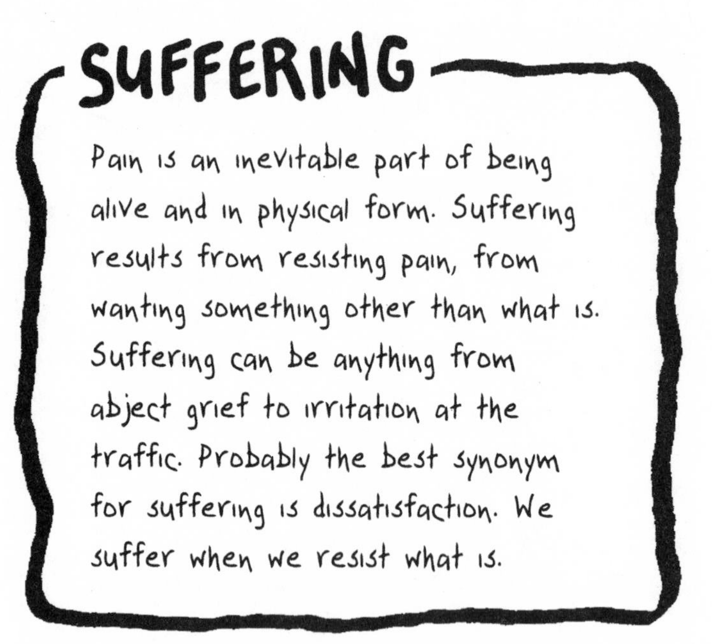

Meditation is a technique for getting HERE. Conditioned mind is a process of, as well as a result of, habitual distraction. Attention flits from thing to thing to thing (thoughts, sensations in the body, emotions, memories, plans, colors, lights, conversations, etc.) while only briefly passing through here/now. Life happens here/now. Everything other than here/now is illusion. The constant pull from a conscious awareness of one's time and place in the present maintains the delusion of other, optional, parallel realities.

Meditation has been practiced throughout the world for thousands of years. In cultures where meditation has been an integral aspect of life, practitioners have learned that sitting in a certain posture - spine straight, body relaxed - is most conducive to being present. Sitting in this position minimizes physical pain and sleepiness.

A MEDITATION POSTURE

Sit on the first one-third of the meditation cushion. If you sit on a meditation bench, stool, or chair, sit well forward. Adjust your leg position until you find one that you can maintain comfortably. Straighten your posture by pushing up from the base of the spine. Imagine that you are trying to touch the ceiling with the crown of your head. As you do this, the chin will tuck slightly and the pelvis will tilt slightly forward. The shoulders and abdomen relax. The eyes are open and unfocused, lowered, and looking at the wall or floor at a 45° angle. The hands are in the cosmic mudra. The right hand is positioned a few inches below the navel, palm up. The left hand, also palm up, rests inside the right hand. The tips of the thumbs touch lightly, forming an oval.

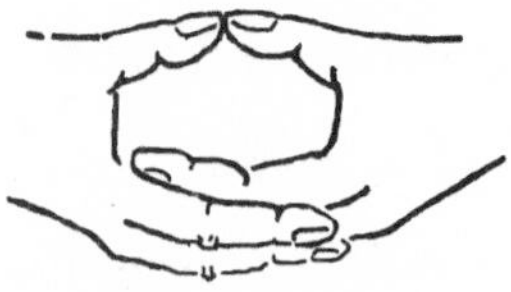

THE BREATH

To stay present and alert in meditation, it can be helpful to focus on the breath. As you sit, breathe naturally and normally. On the first exhalation silently count 1; on the next, count 2; continue until you reach 10; start over at 1. If your attention wanders, gently bring it back and begin again at 1.

Sit for up to 30 minutes. Meditation is not a contest. Being present with yourself for 5 minutes will be much more helpful than beating yourself for 30. If your choice is between a kind meditation and a long one, choose the kind one.

Everything will arise in a meditation practice. If two parts of you are equally committed to "yes" and "no," you can get into an arm-wrestling contest over meditation. As you practice you will see if the part of you saying "no" really doesn't care about meditation but simply wants you to fail. You will also see if the part that says "yes" really does want to meditate or is just attempting to "be the right person."

In meditation you will encounter the conditioning that has been in control of your life. It's not going to say, "Oh, you don't want to suffer anymore? You want to be in charge of your life? You don't want me to make you miserable? OK, no problem." Au contraire! It is going to fight you tooth and nail. Those voices that you always believed were who you are, the ones that are accustomed to being in control, are going to start campaigning against this meditation stuff. My encouragement for you is don't give up. You CAN outlast them. As difficult as it might be to believe when the voices are loudly complaining, your resources are greater. Make a commitment to meditation or anything else, follow through, have something come up to interfere, break your commitment, and commit again! When we're simply present to the whole process, "failure" and "lack of self-discipline" are beside the point. Letting yourself down is beside the point. Being disappointed is beside the point. Feeling discouraged is beside the point. Those reactions are designed to stop you. Recommitting is the point.

If you get talked into quitting, when you wake up, when you remember who you are, get right back to conscious, compassionate awareness. Don't let those voices use awareness against you. If you hear, "Look at you. You quit! You'll never get this. Look how long you've been trying to be aware and you're still a failure at it," realize this is conditioned mind trying to control you - and recommit.

If you pay close attention, you are going to see how a process has been keeping you prisoner. You're going to learn that when you're present in the moment you don't need to fear yourself, anyone, or anything.

A huge part of doing this work
is getting to the point
where it all falls apart.

We don't need to know how to get through the good times! We need to learn what to do when things don't go well, when the voices get the better of us, when we feel like a failure and want to give up. What I hear over and over is that people start something they want to do, do whatever it is, feel great, stop (for reasons they rarely understand), and get the stuffin' beat out of them by their conditioned voices for being a loser and a failure. It's a cycle. It's the universal condition of conditioned humans. The whole thing is designed to go to the point of failure. The whole thing is set up to get to the beating. We are going to see through that, eliminate the beating, and be free of the whole cycle.

Good deal, huh? You are going to stop living in fear that if you're successful and feel good about yourself you'll set off an avalanche of self-hatred. You're going to stop living small in an attempt to avoid beatings.

At a certain point we must,
without self-hatred,
stand at the crossroads,
hear the little voice that says
"You can go in a new direction,"
heed that voice,
and make a choice to end suffering.

Fortunately,
we are at the
crossroads
in each moment,
and the gentle urging
is always with us.

The choice is clear: You can muddle along through life following the voices of conditioning and self-hate as they lead you to more feeling bad, or you can step free of them and be your own person. You can live from center.

I'm encouraging you to find 5 minutes in your day that you're currently wasting and could devote to awareness practice,
meditation,
contemplation,
to something that will lead you to the clear vision of who you are that you're yearning for.

We have plenty of time.
We have plenty of willingness.
We're spending our time on what we're currently spending it on, and we're willing for what we currently have in our lives. We need to check in with exactly how we're spending our time and what it is we're willing for.

A woman told me that each morning she gets up to let her dogs out into the yard for their morning constitutional. She doesn't want to waste time while they're outside so she gets online to check her e-mail. While she's waiting for her server to kick in, she plays a game or two or ten of Solitaire - whatever she can get in before the dogs start barking.

My response? Thank goodness conditioning is helping you not waste time!!!

My suggestion: How about setting up a place from which it is possible to be sensitive to the dogs and away from the temptation of the computer? Just find a chair, sit down, turn your attention to your breath, and notice what happens.

This is about as far away from a waste of time as a person can get!

Life is a tidal wave.

If you wait for things to calm down to start swimming with the current, you might not survive the wait.

Now is the time, and you are equal to the task.

Take the time you would waste listening to self-hate and put that time to good use. If you want to go deeper with this issue, you might decide what time you're going to get up each day for the next month and use that commitment in the 30-day program at the end of this book. It doesn't have to be the same time every day; it could be one time during workdays and another for days off. It could be a different time every day.

It doesn't matter what time you set, only what you do with what you've committed to.

4. Disidentification

- ☆ I want to do something.
- ☆ I do it.
- ☆ I feel good.
- ☆ Voices talk me out of doing it.
- ☆ The same voices beat me up for quitting.

I'll bet all of us can see ourselves in that progression. After the beating (or during) comes the conclusion that what I do or don't do says something about who and how I am. If I don't go to the gym I'm lazy, a slug, an undisciplined loser, hopeless, useless, and headed for an ugly death. Seeing that having those kinds of thoughts is a process, is a pattern, rather than believing the content of the thoughts is true, creates a distance - disidentification - and from that larger perspective, I begin to question the veracity of what I'm being told.

We're learning to accept ourselves exactly as we are. Seeing and accepting ourselves require us to "disidentify" from conditioned mind.

DISIDENTIFICATION

(WHEW!)

Disidentification is stepping back, creating a distance so we can watch conditioned mind instead of being caught in it and believing it. For example, I've decided to begin a meditation practice. As I consider that, I recall how many times I've made that decision and failed. I'm just not a disciplined person. When I stay inside my head with this conversation, it seems like it's just "me" thinking. When I step back and observe the process, I realize conditioned mind is actually telling me who and how I am and what is possible for me. With this disidentification, I can recognize the voice of conditioning and that IT is talking to ME. Disidentification is moving from identification with conditioning to observing conditioning.

As we watch our conditioning, we begin to see how we got where we are in life, and how we get stuck. As we pay attention, we stop believing the content of life - family, money, health, work (another endless list) - and begin to focus on the internal processes that maintain our struggles.

HOW do I suffer?
HOW do I stay stuck?
HOW do I keep winding up in the same place?

CONTENT & PROCESS

CONTENT: The "whats," stuff, issues, problems - the furniture of your life. Job, money, relationship, family, health, possessions - all content. The list is endless.

PROCESS: The "how," the way, the manner, the attitude of mind and heart.

EXAMPLES: Anxiety is a process. What I'm anxious about is the content. Love is a process. What/Who I love is the content.

Conditioned mind
constantly directs our focus
to the content.

Example:
The problem with my relationship is my partner. If only he or she would be different, I would be happy. How can I get my partner to change?

No, no, no! As you have doubtless noticed, that does not get you where you want to go. Better questions would be:

How do I put and keep my partner in the problem position?

What do I believe about relationship?

Which aspects of my personality are involved in the relationship?

What does each of them believe?

What am I projecting onto my partner?

When we're caught by conditioning,
it's "Damned if you do; damned if you don't."

You're in an important meeting. If you say something, it was the wrong thing to say or you didn't express yourself well. If you don't speak up, you're the cause of every wrong thing from that moment forward.

You eat that piece of cake the voice is telling you to eat, and you're called an undisciplined pig as soon as you swallow the last bite. If you don't eat the cake, the voices will convince you that cake was your last hope for happiness and you blew the opportunity.

HUGE freedom comes
when we can hear the voices and not believe them.
They live in their own conditioned reality.
They are projecting.
They are saying what is true for them
and getting you to believe
it has something to do with you.
It doesn't.

When we're present
- when we're disidentified -
we have a whole different relationship
with the voices.
It's when we're not present,
when a small child is listening to
and believing the voices,
that we suffer.

In this practice, Job One is to see through the process that is keeping you from the life that you know is available. An example of the kind of process we are seeing and seeing through: You want to do something, you don't follow through, and you get called a failure with no willpower. Because of your lack of willpower, you can't be successful. But sometimes success happens in spite of the dire predictions of the voices, at which point sabotage kicks in. Soon you have failed once again. "See, I was right, I just can't do it."

The content within that process can be anything. You might want to lose weight, start a meditation practice, stop yelling at the kids, be kinder to your partner, be on time, save money, exercise, keep the house tidier, be more pleasant, drive slower, eat healthier food, find a different job, stop worrying.

You want to start a business; you don't follow through; you get called a failure with no willpower. Because you're a failure with no willpower you can't be successful. If by some chance you have a little success, sabotage kicks in. You begin to overeat or drink too much. You feel anxious and insecure.

Voices of doubt begin to whisper in your ear.

You want to be less irritable with your father. You lay out your plan for being the perfect, loving, understanding son. He starts in with his usual rant, you've had a hard day and lose patience. "See," a voice concludes, "you can't do it. You're weak. You have no resolve. You can't stick with anything. Give it up. You're a failure." If you have a successful time with your father, the voices take another tack: "Oh, sure you did OK this time, but just wait until next time. He'll point out what a disappointment you are, and you'll lose it just like you always do."

Or perhaps your process is less specific: I know I would be happy if only I would (fill in the blank), but I don't stick with it, and so I'm hopeless, and it's all my fault that I'm unhappy.

My examples may not be exact for you, but I bet if you spend a little time looking, you will be able to identify the formula the voices use with you. Once you see how it's done, you will begin to recognize that process being used with every piece of content in your life.

There is no way to appease conditioned mind or self-hate. What you can learn to do is to withdraw your attention from it - disidentify. Moment by moment, bring your attention back to the breath. Give that hateful voice no energy. As difficult as it is to imagine, it has no energy of its own. It has only the energy it can get from you via your participation and resistance. Here's the place to use our nonviolent sit-in training. We sit down, be still, and notice (even when we're going around through the day).

When we don't resist,
when we don't fight or argue or feel bad,
the system cannot maintain itself.

"Duality" holds suffering in place.

DUALITY

This conditioned reality we live in is called the world of opposites. No coin comes without two sides. There is no good without bad, beautiful without ugly, but our conditioning tells us there should be. We suffer when we cling to one side of a duality and reject the other. Acceptance transcends duality. Accepting that life is sometimes this, sometimes that, suffering falls away.

Two subpersonalities get on opposite ends of a duality. They argue and compare while The Judge, as "referee," points out what's wrong with each of them and "you" for having anything to do with them.

Example:
One part of me wants to do something fun that another part of me says I shouldn't. It could be anything, but let's use going away for the weekend for this example.

"I want to go. I need a break," says one part of me. "It's irresponsible. I need to catch up on my work," says another. "You can't even make a simple decision," says The Judge.

When we step back from these parts of ourselves, as we disidentify, and stop believing this kind of conversation has validity, we realize that what "I" am is the conscious, compassionate awareness that sees all of this as it happens.

We learn to stop the torture by turning our attention away from it and toward something else. For me that something else is the breath, the moment, here, where I am.

A good technique for disidentifying: If the voices are very strong, if you feel yourself shrinking and are considering giving up, get out a piece of paper and pen and write down everything the voices say to you. Everything. The voices would like you to believe you won't live that long! Naturally they want you to believe that so you won't do the exercise and prove to yourself that you can outlast them. Keep writing until the feelings dissipate. If they start again, write again. Here's the thing to keep in mind: the less we believe conditioning, the more we step back and see it for what it is, the freer we are.

Watching the process, seeing how it all works, staying focused on awareness rather than getting caught up in "I should...," "I shouldn't...," is the secret. If I'm caught up in the story, believing any of it, trying to be different, I'm miserable. If all those things are going on and I'm just noticing, not believing, not taking it personally, I'm free. Keep in mind this is a process, a practice.

If we meditated daily
and did a quick check-in with ourselves
at the end of the day,

conditioning would have a very hard time
keeping us in bondage.

How do we disidentify?
By any means
that allows us to see our conditioning
rather than be unconsciously controlled by it.

Some helpful disidentification techniques:

☆ Journaling - Write a paragraph about an issue in your life. Write in first person. Example: "I wish my partner would consider my feelings before making a decision that involves me." Then change "I," "me," and "my" to he or she. "She wishes her partner would consider her feelings before making a decision that involves her."

☆ Talking into a tape recorder - The idea here is to then listen to it as if someone else is talking.

☆ Talking to someone who will reflect what we say back to us without giving advice - It is extraordinarily helpful to hear our words reflected back. Often we don't really hear what we just said aloud. (Try it. You'll be amazed.)

☆ Swimming, jogging, walking, etc. - Physical activities help keep our attention in the present, in our bodies, not in the conversation in our heads.

5. Egocentric Karmic Conditioning

Life would be simple if we were comprised of center and a group of subpersonalities. All we would need to do is get to know them, embrace them, meet their needs, and be happy. Alas, it is more complex than that. There is another force operating in our lives, the one I call egocentric karmic conditioning.

EGOCENTRIC KARMIC CONDITIONING

The illusion of a self separate from the rest of life; that illusion's survival system; self-hate; center-of-the-universe-ness; I as subject, everything else as object - these are all synonyms for egocentric karmic conditioning. Example: I drink coffee every morning because I saw my mother do that. If I come from generations of coffee growers, I might be "karmically predisposed" to drink coffee - it's "in my blood." If drinking coffee is an identity for me - the right people drink coffee - I have slipped into the egocentric. What I do, how I am, how I see it is the right/good way.

Here's the part that is so hard to believe it must be experienced directly to be accepted:

Egocentric karmic conditioning
- the illusion of a separate self -
WANTS to suffer.
Why would it want to suffer?
Because suffering makes it "real."
Suffering is how it stays
at the center of the universe.

So it battles to keep you out of center, where the energy and joy of life are available to you, and to trap you into identifying with it.

Someone said to me in an amazed tone of voice, "There are people, voices in my head, talking to me, who don't like me and are mean to me! How did I not notice that?" It is surprising, but in fact most people don't notice the voices until they're pointed out.

SELF-HATE

How did I miss that for all these years?

It's been going on so long, we're so used to the voices, we accept them so unquestioningly, that it's a shock when we finally recognize them. The voices have been there since before we can remember, so it's just "me," just "reality." And saddest of all, we believe those mean things being said are true.

Once we hear the voices,
once we tune in and realize what's going on,
the magnitude of the situation
is such that we can be mortified
that we missed it.

It is essential
that we don't waste time
feeling bad that we were fooled
for so long.

This is our best opportunity to see a lot about how humans operate.

People are missing really obvious stuff all the time.

That's what egocentric karmic conditioning does – it distracts, ignores, and deludes.

Conditioning is simply brainwashing designed to keep us in its imaginary world rather than being present to life as it is.

You see what you're taught
to see,
feel what you're taught
to feel,
hear what you're taught
to hear,
do what you're taught
to do,
and believe what you're taught to believe.

The Voices of Self-Hate

When the survival system that helped you make it through childhood moved from protecting you to protecting itself, self-hate was born. Self-hate is the process egocentric karmic conditioning uses to remain in power.

To free ourselves from self-hate's tyranny, we practice noticing voices talking in our heads, and we pay close attention to who's talking. Is this a subpersonality or is it self-hate? Fortunately we have some clues.

Self-hate is the voice that calls you names,
threatens you, points out your flaws,
tells you what other people are thinking about you,
instills fear,
makes cases against you and others,
and is, in every way, hate-filled.

It is **NASTY**
and **UGLY**
and will do anything to maintain its position of control.

And here is
the most important thing
to know about self-hate:

It is not you!

If a reaction is sincere, if it is coming from a subpersonality who is legitimately upset, it can be reassured. If you say something like, "It's OK, I'm here with you," and the upset abates, you can be pretty sure you're relating with a subpersonality. If, however, you offer the voice reassurance and nothing changes or you hear a hostile reaction, it is very likely conditioning trying to ruin your day.

Aspects of the personality may want anything from ice cream to being voted most popular person in the world, but what they need is unconditional love and acceptance. Getting to center and giving that to yourself (your selves) results in satisfaction and ease. On the other hand, self-hate's interest in satisfaction and ease is highly conditional.

Those voices will declare loudly
that they want to be happy
and at peace,
but don't fall for it.

They may seem content for a short while, but soon a story will start up about what's wrong or missing. "If only this were different, then I'd be happy." If you begin an awareness practice, it won't take you long to discover this for yourself.

When you move to center and offer reassurance, the part of you who is struggling must come into the present to receive the comfort. Egocentric karmic conditioning will not do that, because at center it does not exist. Rather than being comforted, ego will resist and fight, even attack. This is another clue. Subpersonalities tend to be young (even though they can mimic a fairly grown-up conversation). When they are unhappy, perhaps grumpy or uncomfortable, often they are responding to tiredness or hunger. They may be grouchy, but they are not mean. Egocentric karmic conditioning is often hateful.

EXERCISE

What does the voice of self-hate say to you and about you?

Do you believe what it says? If so, what does believing that voice bring to your life?

Can you consider not believing that voice? What would not believing it bring to your life?

Here is a quick look at self-hate/egocentric karmic conditioning in action: You bought this book. You spent good money and went to some effort to obtain it because you want to have a different relationship with some things in your life. So, you get the book and start reading. This is all OK. (There is information in this book that conditioning will be able to use against you, so it has no problem with you reading it.) But suddenly the tables are turning. You're being asked to look at conditioning itself! "Whoa! Wait a darn minute! I don't like this. I don't want to do this. This is stupid. This is a waste of time." Now, who do you think is talking? Your heart? Your authentic nature? The part of you who wants not to suffer? The part of you who wants to be free to enjoy life?

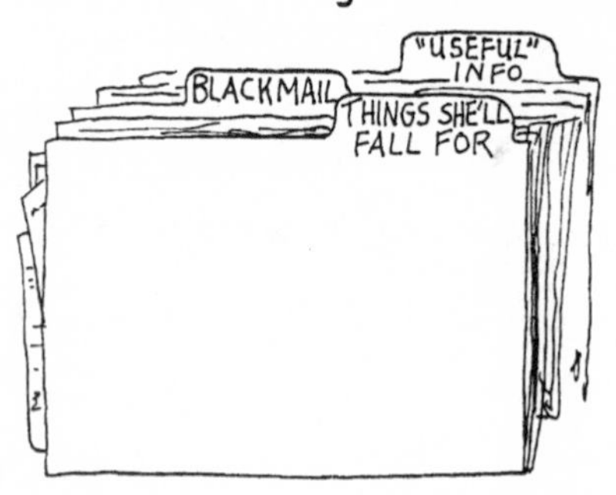

As you listen to the voice complaining and resisting, be aware that you are, in fact, listening. You are not talking! A voice is making a case for not reading this book and you are listening to it! It has fooled you in the past because you were not paying close enough attention to see that it was talking and you were listening. You thought "you" were "it."

Conditioning has as many ways to protect itself as there are people. I hear things like "It feels weird to have conversations with parts of myself," or "It feels wrong to divide myself into subpersonalities," and "I feel sorry for those hateful voices." Again, don't fall for it. Those are scams self-hate runs to defend itself from being exposed as the

joy-stealing,
energy-draining,
life-robbing
trickster it is.

Do you know the expression, "One definition of insanity is doing the same thing over and over and expecting a different result"? If you want to do the same thing you've always done - that is, if you want to continue believing what the voices tell you - then you're going to stay where you are.

You'll make an enthusiastic commitment to
lose weight,
stop smoking,
exercise,
go back to school...
(add your own),
and everything will go well for a while.

Eventually, the voices will start campaigning that
it's all too hard,
and when the voices tell you to,
you'll stop...

...and then they will beat you up for stopping.
You will do your best to be the right person,
and the voices will shame you
for not meeting the standard.
You can count on it.

We NOTICE all of this,
but we don't BELIEVE any of it.

Believing and noticing are not the same thing. Believing the voices will result in doing the same thing and getting the same result. Noticing will enable you to see: Who gets grumpy? Who doesn't eat right? Who has physical problems? Who doesn't care? Who is invested in maintaining the status quo?

Paying attention enables you to see
how you get distracted,
how you get fooled,
how you end up in the same suffering place
over and over.

It is important to listen to everything that goes on inside your head, but you don't need to get caught up in it. It's like listening to the propaganda spread by a corrupt government. You listen so you can know what they're up to. You don't listen so you can join in their game.

We listen and notice and watch and pay attention
to egocentric karmic conditioning
so we can see how we are controlled,
how we are stopped from doing what we want to do,
how we are kept from being as we want to be.

Who are the players?
Who do they talk to?
What do they say?
What happens when we believe them?

We listen and watch and pay attention
without needing to change anything.

We observe and write it all down
until the whole system
of conditioned suffering
becomes OBVIOUS
and is no longer believable.

6. Mentoring: Kind and Wise Support

It is my theory that until we learn to take care of ourselves, our lives are in the hands of egocentric karmic conditioning.

In *There Is Nothing Wrong With You*, I make the point, over several pages in an increasingly loud voice (larger print), that

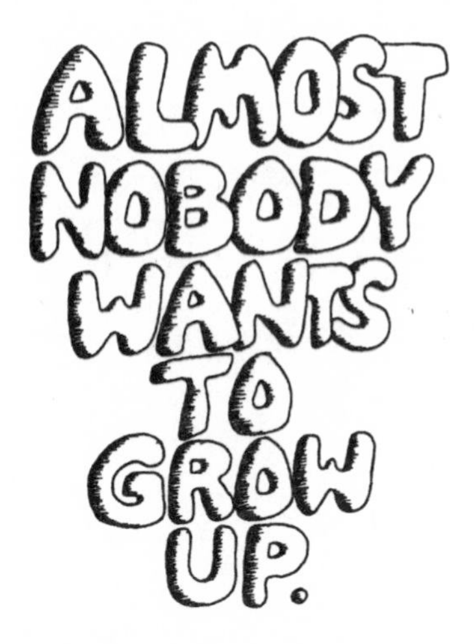

In awareness practice "growing up" takes a whole new direction.

Not only will you be a "grown-up" in the sense of taking responsibility for yourself and life, you will do it from consciousness and compassion. You will be "the Buddha," the awakened one, making centered choices in the moment rather than remaining stuck in conditioned reactions from the past.

This is a better approach to life than the ever-popular strategy of manipulating someone else into taking care of you!

As the bumper sticker says:

Now the work is to take each of those young "yous" by the hand, pull them into your lap, and be the person they've always hoped would be there to guide them through life with unconditional love and acceptance. Now you have the opportunity to mentor those children in the way they (you) were not the first time around.

That's why meditation is so important. In meditation we find the center of conscious, compassionate awareness, and from that place mentor the young parts of ourselves who never had anyone help them understand their wants and needs.

The Mentor I'm encouraging you to find is not a source of permissive self-indulgence. Nor is the

Mentor a hard taskmaster who makes you do stuff you don't want to do for your own good. The Mentor speaks from conscious, compassionate awareness. The Mentor, being center, loves you and all life unconditionally.

Ego has no interest in mentoring. For that reason I encourage people to put up signs, write notes, get tattoos - ANYTHING to help bring them to consciousness.

When you're HERE, you're with the Mentor.

Show appreciation to yourself for the efforts you're making to do this work. Give yourself some little rewards:

Some pats on the back (an argument for a yoga practice)

A message of congratulations or thanks on your computer or voice mail

An appreciation card

Tickets to a play

The trip of your dreams

You know, the kind of things you would do for someone you care about.

We'd all like to have someone who thinks we're wonderful, encourages us, and loves us unconditionally. We can be with that person all the time because we have that person inside us.

The relationship with the Mentor is like any other relationship: we make it strong in the easy times so it can sustain us through the hard times. Practice will make all the difference.

Self-Coaching

In the old days coaches trained people via self-hatred. "Inspiration through humiliation." Boys were sometimes motivated by calling them the most humiliating thing imaginable: girls. Nowadays we have modern coaches who use many of the techniques

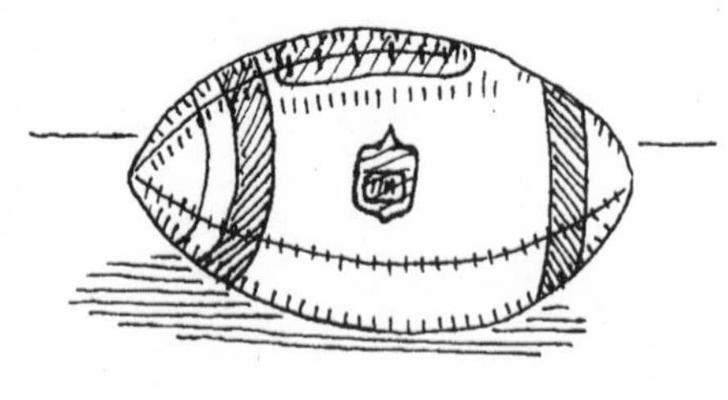

we're applying here: encouragement, mentoring, praise, and support. Guess what? People respond better to kindness than cruelty. Why, it's even caught on in the workplace, that bastion of self-hatred and disrespect.

There are three helpful things to keep in mind as we move from being identified with conditioned to becoming our own mentor:

1. how little we teach children about how things work and what things mean,

2. how much adults assume about what children understand, and

3. what advantage self-hate takes of that fact.

So much of what passes for education is nothing more than adults inflicting their unexamined beliefs and assumptions onto children and projecting their own unexamined reasons and motivations onto children's reactions. Parents often forget that children do not know what the parents know, have not had the experience the parents have had. For instance, children don't understand what money is or what it means or how stressful it can be for adults to get and keep enough money. Children don't have bills or hold jobs or worry about old age or retirement. In fact, it's quite a while before children actually know that money doesn't grow on trees. Bananas do. Why not money? For a child the world is a huge unknown. Every aspect of life is brand new. (It is for each of us, but as adults we've mostly forgotten this.) Instead of a parent or teacher taking a step-by-step approach to "the how of learning," most children get the stumble-through-and-figure-it-out-for-yourself-in-pain-and-suffering approach. "I have already told you that!" means little to a child confronting a vast array of new information with no clues about what is important to focus on.

Some years ago while doing some workshops at an outdoor center, I was invited to learn to kayak. Now, I'm not overly fond of water and would never have approached kayaking of my own volition, but since I began teaching awareness practice - a natural love of mine - I have made it a practice to take up new activities, usually physical, that are not easy for me so I can stay in touch with what it's like to learn new, potentially scary stuff.

So, there we were, sitting in an eddy, reading the river (which was utterly lost on me), and getting ready to paddle across to the other side. My instructor, a world-class white-water competitor and instructor (yes, she was in the Olympics), began taking me through all the information I would need to get from here to there. Okay, okay, yeah, okay, got it.

Ready? My head is nodding yes while every muscle in my body has locked into NO.

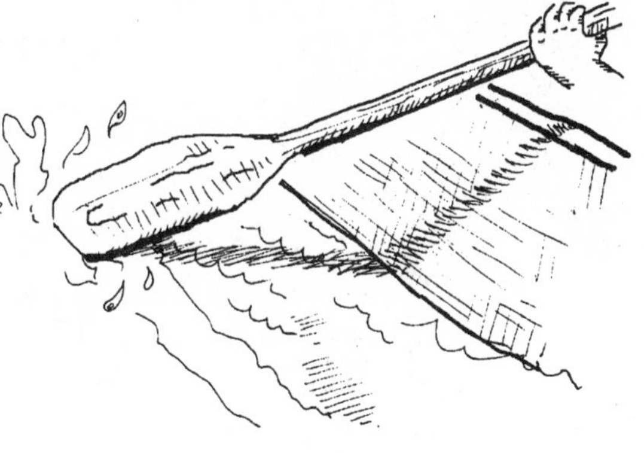

Divine intervention must have kept me in that little boat because my performance was something less than stellar. I got several more tips. The next trip was worse. Finally, as we pulled into another eddy and I pantingly got my little craft turned in the right direction, I asked my teacher to tell me the three most important things for me to know in this moment. I realized there was no context into which I could integrate theory or philosophy or contingency plans. I needed one place to focus my attention and two other places to be aware of. That's all! As I mastered those I could sense the next step as she offered it, and then the next.

At the Zen Monastery Peace Center in Murphys, California, when a person arrives for a period of monastic training, they are immediately given a job outside their area of expertise...

They are asked to do this task in a very specific way and are guided to perform the task precisely as requested. They are closely supervised and allowed no independent decisions - what we call "better ideas." This accomplishes several marvelous objectives once the person moves past the horror of feeling about three years old in a grown-up world.

--The student does not have to be smart, clever, knowledgeable, or a high achiever.

--The student can let go of all other concerns and simply be present to a simple task.

--The student gets to see and hear all the conditioning that is in the way of being present in the moment.

--The student gets to move out of the head and into the body.

--And most important of all, the student gets to learn how to learn.

The Monastery exists because it is critical that this transformative work happen in a safe, "privileged" environment. As the student practices, usually feeling like a small child, hearing the voices of conditioned fear, anger, judgment, and self-hatred, they are encouraged to move into the role of mentor with the part of themselves they have always identified as "I," but that they have come to realize is a very young aspect of their personality. Now they are in a position to change the past and alter the future.

In the present, we can undo the past and release the future through bringing conscious, compassionate awareness to that in us that suffers. The specific process of ending suffering from the past is to embrace in compassion the aspects of ourselves who were injured by unconscious conditioning, thereby freeing them from identification with an experience from the past and enabling them to move into the present, into acceptance and kindness.

7. Self-Discipline and Eating

Eating is often a source of great suffering. What and how much to eat are questions we face every day. If we are conscious, there is no problem. At a retreat a woman said, "I've noticed that I can generally maintain my commitment to lose a few extra pounds as long as I maintain conscious awareness while eating." This is a huge piece of the puzzle.

"Going unconscious" is the reaction to specific triggers. Rising energy that gets labeled "tension" is one of those triggers. A series of connections begins that takes the unaware person down a path of bad decisions. For instance, I am conditioned to ignore early warning signs of hunger. I'm busy, I'm involved in something important, and I avoid signals of growling stomach and dropping blood sugar. I can never remember to bring a snack or to avoid coffee and sugar when I won't be able to eat for several hours. Soon I am miserable. Inside I'm hysterical. I can't focus or concentrate, and I hate everyone around me. When I finally get to food,

I stuff myself with the quickest, easiest items I can get my hands on. I pack in way more empty calories than I need before my brain gets information about how much I've ingested. Alas, fast food is designed for the person in my condition. Snack foods are made for people in blood sugar crisis.

So, we want to bring conscious, compassionate awareness to the issue of food. Someone - probably someone who rarely gets what she or he needs (a diet that feels good) - wants to bring consciousness to a suffering relationship with food. Let's say the person who came up with this decision to be more conscious doesn't want to eat junk food. Now, this is not an unreasonable desire, wanting not to eat things that just about everyone except those selling the junk agrees is not good for you. It is not unreasonable to want support in being healthier.

But another someone (egocentric karmic conditioning) is threatened by this desire. Why would that be so? Because eating, along with every addiction we struggle with, is not about the content, it is about the process, and the process is identity maintenance. Who would I be if I had a kind, compassionate relationship with food? What would happen to self-hatred if I ate what was good for me and was healthy and felt good about myself? There would be no drama! There would be no suffering. There would be no egocentric karmic conditioning to control me. And egocentric karmic conditioning is not going to give up without a fight!

So, now that the fight is on, rules and willpower and forcing and "denying myself" are introduced. It can no longer be a simple matter of a decision not to eat junk food. It's a contest in which "I" will "make myself do what I don't want to do." But who is this "myself"? This is not the person who wants to feel better through avoiding junk food. Suddenly the desire to eat healthy food has become a matter of failure and screwing up and feeling bad. Who is the "I" behind this? It is egocentric karmic conditioning trying to turn the success of eating well and feeling good into failure and misery. Picture this: You have a friend who is having health issues and suspects he would feel better not eating junk food. Could you be supportive? Would it need to be about punishment and misery and deprivation and poor me? Of course not. If that were someone you loved, you would be coming up with healthy recipes, finding restaurants that serve delicious, nutritious choices, and encouraging tasty, healthy snacks.

The secret is to disidentify from the conditioning and start seeing ourselves as someone we love. When I no longer believe I need to or deserve to be beaten or mistreated or spoken to cruelly, I will stop believing the self-hating voices, and I will stop the behaviors that are not good for me. Overeating, eating junk, rewarding or punishing myself with food aren't compassionate, and the unconscious behaviors are done precisely because they are not compassionate.

If you can stay conscious as the energy increases, if you can remain present to the sensations in your body rather than believing they mean you need to do something, you can sidestep the conditioned behaviors. That is a good argument for learning to pay close attention through the practice of meditation.

Conscious eating

"Conscious eating" can be done in many ways. Here are a few:

Put your fork down between bites.

Bow between bites.

Chew each bite 50 times.

Chew 50 times, and then bow before taking another bite.

Do not do anything other than eat while eating.

There are lots of fun variations.

You might hear voices beginning to grumble and complain. "This is too hard. This isn't any fun. It'll be boring." If you are tempted to believe them, recall how little fun it is to overeat, to be overweight, to feel like an undisciplined failure, to listen to the voices going on about how you look and what it says about you that you have eating issues. Here's the thing: If you love food, be present to eating. Smell the food, look at it, eat with your hands if you like, so you can feel it, take little bites and chew them a lot so you can savor every morsel. Make it last. Let it be sensual. Make it a feast - a feast for one. A party for you.

The voices want you to gobble your food without knowing what and how much you ate, and then they want you to feel bad and dissatisfied afterward. Don't fall for it.

The easiest way for me to see compassionate self-discipline around food is to think of an adored child. I want that child to be happy, creative, spontaneous, free, adventuresome, and as safe as I can help her be. But, as with most children, as soon as she discovers sugar, it becomes the food group of choice. If I love that child I'm not going to let her eat sugar all day. She'd get sick. She'd be unhealthy. Loving that child means I'm going to take responsibility for showing up, being present, and offering the best food guidance I can.
Does this mean you will never again get to eat a

piece of cake or candy? No, of course not. It means you will eat it when it is good for you to eat it, not when it's an unconscious decision from self-hate. Let's say I commit to eating a limited amount of sugar once per day. I know sugar isn't good for me, I don't feel well, I weigh more than is comfortable, and I feel totally out of control with the issue. Because I'm used to eating a lot of sugar every day, the stress is going to build. Voices start angling for their sugar. Conditioning starts distracting, making cases, dropping stupid dust, making deals.

STUPID DUST

Stupid dust is the illusion of confusion. Suddenly you can't remember what self-discipline is or why you ever thought it was a good idea or just exactly what is compassion anyway? It's a variation on the old "You are getting very sleepy..." as conditioning stupefies you and lulls you into unconsciousness. Even very intelligent people periodically get sprinkled with stupid dust.

The Judge starts expressing an opinion about who and how I am for having an issue with sugar in the first place. I watch it all. I breathe and observe and write down everything that goes on. I am practicing staying at center, disidentified, not drawn into the fray. I am practicing choosing compassion over self-hatred. I am addressing the issue. I'm cutting back on sugar. I'm taking responsibility for my health and well-being, and I'm doing it from the place that is most compassionate to all. Compassion for the sugar addict, compassion for the habit, compassion for the body, compassion for the opinions, compassion for the person who wants to be free of the addiction.

8. Self-Discipline and Time Management

How do you apply compassionate self-discipline to time management?

The issue of time management can include
punctuality,
use of time,
ability to focus,
distraction,
setting priorities,
organization...
add your own.

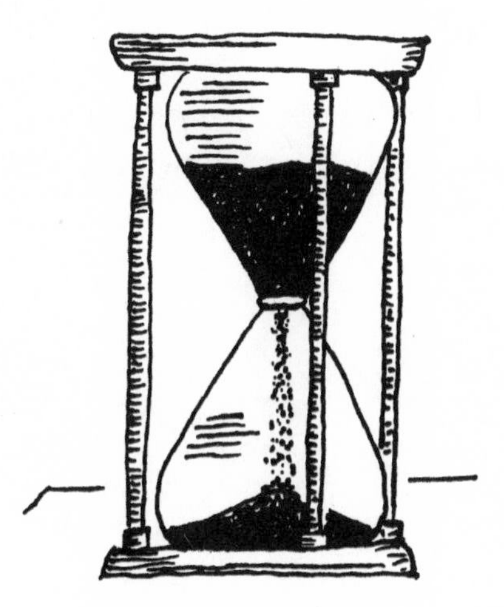

Perhaps you are a person who is always punctual. Perhaps that trait is in the category of "how people should be" and you feel good about it. We're taught to believe there is no reason to pay attention to areas in which we are doing well.

But in this practice we are focused on ending suffering, so I would ask you to consider the effect punctuality has on your life, and I don't mean only *your* punctuality.

Yes, you feel right and like a good person for being on time, but how do you feel about others who are not punctual?

How do you treat people when they are late?

And what happens with you when you are unable to be on time?

Or perhaps

you're the

person who

never seems

to be on

time.

Do you know how you manage to do that?

What are the steps you take that make you late most of the time?

What do you believe about yourself as a person who is late?

What do the voices in your head say about you?

What do you project others think about you?

EXERCISE

To see more clearly, take a few moments and jot down what you see about your relationship with time.

Perhaps you're hearing voices (probably calm, logical voices) letting you know that you really don't have time for this kind of stuff. Introspection is good and helpful, of course, but there just isn't time right now. Maybe later when... the kids are grown? You've retired? You've died of old age?

The truth is, you can't afford NOT to "waste time" on this kind of stuff!!!

Conditioning is working hard to ruin your life.

You must work at least as hard not to let it.

The rewards are enormous.

9. Self-Discipline vs. Self-Improvement

Compassionate self-discipline has nothing to do with self-improvement.

Self-improvement
comes from conditioning you received as a child,
is based on a false premise
(that there is something wrong with you),
and results in suffering.
(Zen is a path of ending suffering.)

So please put aside all ideas of changing and improving yourself, at least until you see where those ideas came from, until you're sure who all the players are.

Ask yourself:
--"Who" in me (which aspect of my personality) thinks I need to be improved?
--"Who" thinks she or he knows how to do that?
--Has self-improvement worked so far?

People try to "fix" us when we are children. Their motives might be good - they want us to be safe and socially acceptable (it's what was done to them) - and now, as adults, we've taken on the job ourselves. The part of you who feels you should improve was trained by those who tried to fix you as a child.

So, before we worry about improving, let's find the part of you that those well-meaning souls were working on.

Can you find inside yourself the trying-really-hard little person who just wanted to be good and do it right? That's the person I want you to spend some time with and get to know. It can be helpful to pull out pictures of yourself around the ages of three to five. Look into the eyes of that child and see if she or he needs anything other than unconditional love and compassionate guidance.

10. Awareness Practice

We call this work "awareness practice." Awareness practice unveils that which keeps us from a natural state of ease and acceptance and joy. We bring the assumptions, lies, illusions, and fantasies of conditioned mind into the light, revealing the delusions that run our lives, that imprison us in suffering.

As you begin the daily meditation and nightly review - parts of "30 Days of Compassionate Self-Discipline" - remember that the point is not to succeed or fail, not to be a good person for doing it right or a bad person for doing it wrong, but just to see what happens,

to reveal how suffering is caused
by our relationship with conditioned mind.

Guided Retreat

***

30 Days of Compassionate Self-Discipline

DAY 1

This 30-day guided retreat is, at bottom, basic training in awareness practice. We will bring awareness to compassionate self-discipline. Within that, you will choose an aspect of your life with which to practice compassionate self-discipline. As you do these daily exercises and practices, you will learn how to pay attention. You will develop the ability to turn your attention to any aspect of life, see how you are causing yourself to suffer, embrace that in compassion, and end the suffering.

You need two things for this retreat: a journal and a place to meditate. These can be as simple or as fancy as you like.

About meditation (see chapter three, "Meditation," to review how to sit): If you are new to meditation, please don't allow the voices (which are attempting to get you NOT to meditate) to turn your meditation into a contest. You can sit on a comfortable chair or in full-lotus; you can sit for 5 minutes or 30. Meditation is not an endurance contest - enjoy it! The voices of self-hate, failure, punishment, and humiliation want you to believe that you succeed only if you are miserable but manage to endure. (Which won't count, anyway, because you will have committed some other crime or sin such as "not really wanting to.") So, since according to the conditioned voices you will never succeed anyway, go on ahead and make this manageable. As you learn to enjoy meditation - which you will with this approach - you will meditate for longer times and probably choose new postures that feel better to you as your practice deepens. For now, less is more.

YOUR ASSIGNMENT: Decide where you will sit and what you will use for your journal. In your journal write your answers to these questions:

1) What does "self-discipline" mean to you?
2) What is your history with self-discipline?

An Encouragement

You might quit this program a hundred times before you finish it. That's not a problem. In fact, that would be a good thing. Quit and then recommit just as soon as you realize you've quit. If you do the exercises each time you recommit, your ability to pay attention and your understanding will simply continue to expand. You could start this guided retreat at the beginning of the month, do it to completion, start again at the beginning of the next month *for the rest of your life* and your life would be completely transformed. So whenever the voices talk you into quitting, notice everything about how that happens: what they say, what you believe, how you feel, what happens in your body, what choices you make while under the direction and influence of the voices. Then start the retreat at Day 1 as soon as you wake up and realize what happened.

DAY 2

Choose something - a personal issue, problem, or concern - with which to practice compassionate self-discipline for the duration of this guided retreat. It doesn't matter what you choose. We are practicing with PROCESS, and the CONTENT is largely irrelevant. Examples of "content" you might practice with: junk food, alcohol, exercise, children, spouse, patience, work, procrastination, punctuality, stress, emotions, temper, responsibility, money, sex, gratitude, shopping, listening, defensiveness, control, saying no, guilt, fear, anxiety, gluttony, etc.

Choose something that is not your biggest issue. As we practice with less charged content, we have an opportunity to see the same process that conditioning uses to dictate our quality of life with the big issues. If you have difficulty exercising, but not nearly as much difficulty as with junk food, choose exercising. If alcohol is a huge issue, but procrastination shows up on a daily basis, pick procrastination. It's easier to see the process self-hate is using when we have fewer beliefs about the importance of the issue. Because we are working with a process, once you see how this works, you will be able to apply the principles to any content in your life.

YOUR ASSIGNMENT: Decide how long you will sit each morning and write that down. Choose what you commit to practicing compassionate self-discipline with for this retreat and write that down. Write these in big letters (bright and colorful if you're feeling creative) and make a "commitment poster." Hang it where you will see it first thing each morning. Put it with the journal you're going to use at the end of each day to chart your "Adventures in Awareness."

DAY 3

Look at what you have chosen to work with for this guided retreat to see if it is a clear, compassionate, specific, and measurable goal. In other words, "I want to lose weight" is not specific or measurable. It might be clear, and how you approach achieving the goal may be compassionate, but it will be very difficult to know when you've achieved it. Will five pounds be enough to qualify? Will you get messages of failure even after losing fifty pounds if you're sixty pounds over your ideal weight? Perhaps a more compassionate, clear, specific, and measurable goal would be to decide to cut your consumption of sweets to once a day, 5 days per week while adding 30 minutes of exercise 4 days per week. If you have decided to work on procrastination, you might decide to complete a project you have been postponing. Remember, this is a PROCESS we're bringing conscious, compassionate awareness to. You will be seeing HOW you procrastinate or overeat or don't meditate.

If you don't have something in particular to practice with (and even if you do), you can practice with this guided retreat itself because you have committed to the daily meditation.

YOUR ASSIGNMENT: Beginning today, please complete this "Daily Evening Review":

1) Did you meditate this morning? If the answer is "yes," how did that happen? If "no," what stopped you?

2) What insights or awarenesses did you have today?

DAY 4

Attention moves in a field of awareness. As you're reading this, notice that your attention is on the words on the page, yet you can be aware of the activity in the mind as the words are turned into meanings and the information processed. Perhaps you can sense attention moving back and forth between the words on the page and the activity in the mind. Then you may notice that you want to stop and "take this in." Perhaps your gaze leaves the words on the page and moves to the middle distance. Perhaps your eyes go slightly out of focus, and your attention and awareness are taken up with your thoughts.

You might have noticed this process in other areas of your life. You're driving down the road with your attention moving back and forth between what's around you and the activity inside the mind. You notice the other cars or stores or pedestrians, then you're planning a meeting or reviewing a conversation or deciding what to have for dinner.

YOUR ASSIGNMENT: Notice the interplay between attention and awareness during your meditation and throughout the day. Complete your Daily Evening Review.

DAY 5

How are you doing with your commitment? Perhaps already you have not kept your commitment to the content you're working with, or maybe you've not done the daily meditation or review. Whether you did them or not is irrelevant. What matters is seeing HOW you do not keep your agreements.

YOUR ASSIGNMENT: Begin to jot down the conversation in your head about your commitments. What is the self-talk you're hearing? Do you hear comments such as "This is too hard," "You're too busy," "You're not going to make it through 30 days anyway, why don't you just quit now?" If the conversation is upbeat and enthusiastic, write that down too. Write down as much of the conversation as you are aware of, especially when the point of it is to get you NOT to write down the self-talk! Complete your Daily Evening Review.

DAY 6

We have the ability to experience ourselves as separate from life. We can imagine that life could be or should be different from the way it is. We are conditioned to believe that we can control life (if you were the right person, you could make life be the way you want it to be, the way it SHOULD be). These are illusions, but we experience them as very REAL illusions. None of those beliefs is a problem except that, to the degree we believe them to be true, we suffer.

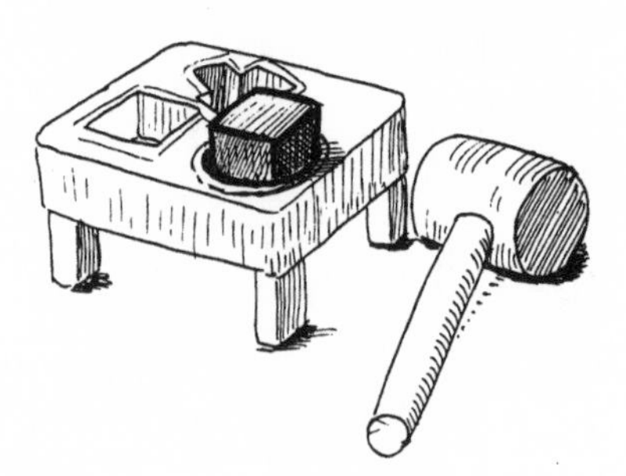

YOUR ASSIGNMENT: Notice how much of the conversation in your head is in support of unexamined beliefs. A good technique for this exploration is to ask the question "Is that so?" or "How do you know that?" each time you hear an opinion, judgment, or statement of fact go through your head. For instance, if you hear comments such as "He is so selfish" or "I can't stand this," it would be helpful to ask the person making those comments to tell you HOW those conclusions were reached. Complete your Daily Evening Review.

DAY 7

Before a fair amount of introspection reveals something different, we believe that we are a single, unified entity. I'm me. "I" am "me." I think my thoughts and feel my feelings. Upon closer examination we begin to notice that there is more than one "I" making up "me." As you watch your process around bringing compassionate self-discipline to the content you chose for this guided retreat, notice which aspects of the personality are involved. Certainly you have one personality who wants to succeed. There may be others who do not. Fit-and-Trim wants to go to the gym; Couch Potato has no interest. Patient Parent has all the willingness in the world; No-Time-for-Myself just wants to get away.

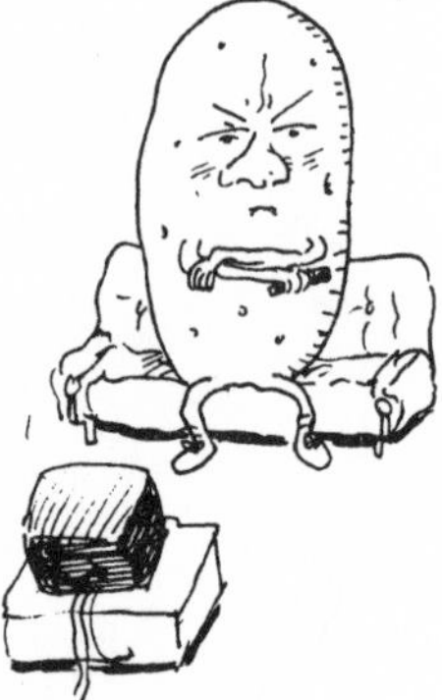

YOUR ASSIGNMENT: Write descriptions of and draw pictures of the subpersonalities who are involved in your commitment. Complete your Daily Evening Review.

DAY 8

Perhaps the most critical (in every sense of the word) player in any attempt to make a change in your life is The Judge. For most people, The Judge came into existence as an attempt to get information about what they were doing wrong before other people had a chance to point it out. Small children live in a world of "doing it wrong." They don't know what people want them to do or how to do what people want them to do. For a lot of folks, the learning process is quite brutal. You can hear the voice of The Judge in self-talk such as "You'd better not!" or "You're going to get in trouble." After listening awhile, you can often detect the tone of one small child chastising or threatening another.

YOUR ASSIGNMENT: Write down the self-talk from The Judge. Find or draw a picture of this subpersonality. Complete your Daily Evening Review.

DAY 9

Because identifying "who the players are" is such a crucial aspect of awareness practice, let's look further at "who's talking."

YOUR ASSIGNMENT: Today, focus on the self-talk from the part of you who wants to keep your commitment. As you are doing so, you will probably hear comments made by the parts of you who do NOT want you to keep your commitment. Notice what The Judge has to say. See if there are other players you haven't been aware of. Write it all down. Complete your Daily Evening Review.

DAY 10

Many of us grow up convinced that punishment, or fear of it, makes and keeps people good. Guilt and remorse are signs that we know right from wrong and feel bad about the bad things we've done. Bad and wrong get all tangled up in childish thinking, and we find people unable to distinguish degrees of culpability, or even to see when an action or thought is not wrong or bad but simply unhelpful. The person who eats an extra piece of cake may be punished (internally) as severely as if they had committed a crime. A person slights a coworker or friend and is overwhelmed by guilt and remorse.

YOUR ASSIGNMENT: Notice how often conditioned mind scans for examples and proof of your wrongdoing. Notice how you feel when a voice brings charges of wrongdoing against you or takes you through, step by step, over and over again, one of your alleged sins or crimes. Complete your Daily Evening Review.

DAY 11

There's a good chance that with all this paying attention to the voices in your head, you are able to distinguish self-hating voices. Name-calling, mean and cruel statements about who and how you are - the kinds of things you would never say to or about someone you care about - are examples of self-hatred.

YOUR ASSIGNMENT: Begin to make a list of those comments that could in no way be characterized as helpful - the ones that are self-hatred making you feel bad. Add to the list every time you hear a self-hating comment go through your head. Complete your Daily Evening Review.

DAY 12

If you are willing to consider that punishment is not what makes people good but, in fact, contributes to self-hating choices, begin to consider what kind of appreciation system you are going to implement to replace the self-hate, judgment, and punishment conditioning has been using to control you. What makes you feel appreciated? What makes you feel loved? When you do a good job, what do you want to hear? What do you say to someone you care about to let that person know you appreciate him or her?

YOUR ASSIGNMENT: Choose an "appreciation mantra" ("You're doing a great job." "You're my hero." "Thank you for all your hard work.") and figure out how you are going to remember to say this to yourself (silently is fine, aloud is better!) at least 10 times today. And say it! Complete your Daily Evening Review.

DAY 13

Remember, this is awareness practice. These questions and exercises are designed to help you see how conditioned mind causes suffering. You are not doing this to get it "right." So, watch everything that arises as you read the assignments. We're seeing how suffering is maintained and learning to step back and be free of old beliefs, stories, viewpoints, and behaviors. You cannot do this wrong! Here's the thing to keep in mind: The more present, aware, and conscious you are, the more egocentric karmic conditioning will squawk. The best way for it to get you to go unconscious is to pull you into a conversation about what's wrong. Don't fall for it!

YOUR ASSIGNMENT: Step back and get a sense of how you're doing thus far. What are you seeing? Are the voices heating up? Are you being talked into distractions? Perhaps you're falling for the voices that are talking you into MORE of the very behaviors you're doing this retreat to overcome! Even so, are you more present to your daily life? Complete your Daily Evening Review.

DAY 14

The only thing that doesn't want us to be free and happy is egocentric karmic conditioning, ego, "I," the illusion of a separate self, conditioned mind. (When you hear moaning, groaning, whining, and complaining, you'll know who's talking to you.) The best antidote to conditioning, to self-hatred, is kindness. Why is that so? Because kindness comes from center, from the heart.

YOUR ASSIGNMENT: Do something kind for yourself today. Jot down what you think, feel, and believe about your choice. Complete your Daily Evening Review.

DAY 15

Tie a string around your finger (wear a different bracelet, put your watch on the other wrist, put your ring on a different finger, wear a different cap to help you remember to take little "snapshots" of yourself throughout the day. Each time you remember, each time you are HERE, conscious and present, for even a moment, check in to see who you are and how you are.

YOUR ASSIGNMENT: Notice which subpersonalities you are aware of identifying with today. On the whole, were you judgmental of yourself or were you kind to yourself? Complete your Daily Evening Review.

DAY 16

Keep in mind that NOTHING is outside awareness. How you respond to the assignments, how you make the commitment, how you write it out, how you come up with your journal, where you put it, every voice you hear, all the aspects of the personality who slip in and out offering opinions - ALL OF IT will give you the clues you're looking for on the road to freedom. You're an explorer, a sleuth, the Indiana Jones of awareness. Pay attention to everything, don't believe anything, and don't take anything personally. The odds are very good that this mission will get treacherous before it's over. You are absolutely qualified for the job. What is the job? To learn to be a nonstop, full-time, unconditionally loving and accepting mentor to the person whose birthright is freedom, and who has mistakenly agreed to believe him or herself unworthy.

YOUR ASSIGNMENT: Ask the Mentor to give you some words of encouragement about how you're doing. Here's a little hint about accessing your Mentor: Pretend that you are going to give feedback to a young person you love unconditionally. The kinds of things you would say to that young person are the kinds of things the Mentor will say to you. Complete your Daily Evening Review.

DAY 17

After a period of meditation, spend a few minutes practicing *being* the Mentor. Ask any struggling parts of you to let you know how they feel and what kind of help they need. Perhaps write down the conversation in your journal, using the dominant hand for the Mentor and the nondominant hand for the subpersonality.

We'd all like to have someone who thinks we're wonderful, encourages us, and loves us unconditionally. We can be with that person all the time because we have that person inside us.

YOUR ASSIGNMENT: Toward the end of your day, practice mentoring a part of you who is having a hard time. Complete your Daily Evening Review.

DAY 18

The Buddha taught that we each have one person to save - ourselves. We are each capable of being the conscious, compassionate awareness that ends suffering. Compassionate self-discipline is a big part of the "how" of ending suffering.

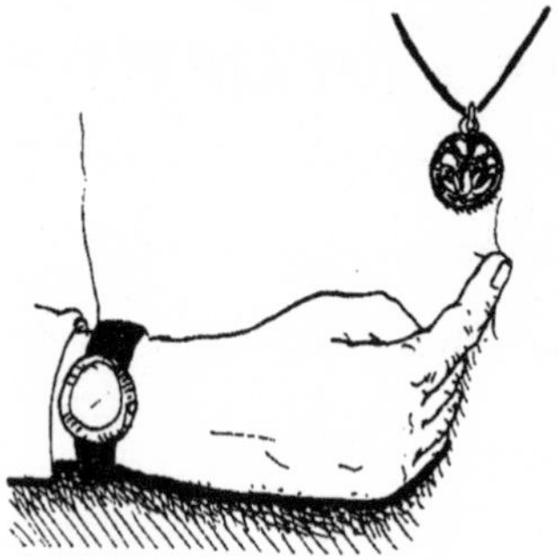

YOUR ASSIGNMENT: Notice the places in your life in which kindness is lacking. Choose one to begin bringing kindness to for the rest of this retreat. Complete your Daily Evening Review.

DAY 19

The Mentor I'm encouraging you to find is not a source of permissive self-indulgence, nor a hard taskmaster who makes you do stuff you don't want to do for your own good.

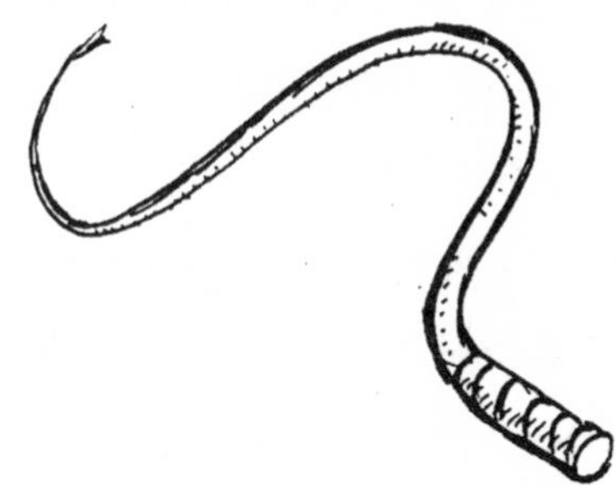

The Mentor speaks from conscious, compassionate awareness. The Mentor, being center, loves you and all life unconditionally. The Mentor is the process of compassionate self-discipline.

YOUR ASSIGNMENT: Ask the Mentor about the relationship between kindness and self-discipline. Complete your Daily Evening Review.

DAY 20

It may be that at this point in your program it would be helpful to revise your commitment. Perhaps you took on too much. Maybe your goal was not specific enough. Or it could be that you feel complete with the issue you chose and feel ready to make another commitment. Perhaps conditioned mind is using one of these arguments for sabotaging the plan you made on Day 1.

YOUR ASSIGNMENT: See where you are with your commitment and with the program. Make a plan to continue, wholeheartedly, with the commitment you made for these 30 days, knowing you can work with something new, different, larger, or smaller when you begin again. Extra-credit assignment: watch what you do instead of being the Mentor. Complete your Daily Evening Review.

DAY 21

As you have no doubt realized throughout a lifetime of resolutions and self-improvement projects, willpower lacks staying power. We can get inspired and fired up to make some sort of personality change, and then, often in a shockingly short time, we run out of steam.

Once you comprehend compassionate self-discipline, you will no longer have to rely on inspiration or willpower to accomplish what you want to do. You will have more than tools and techniques to make changes or obtain results; you will have an attitude of mind and heart that makes just about anything in life available to you.

YOUR ASSIGNMENT: Write down what you see as the differences between compassionate self-discipline and inspiration/resolutions/willpower. Complete your Daily Evening Review.

DAY 22

Everyone, from small children to puppies to you and me, appreciates recognition and praise. Everyone wants a sense of belonging and to feel that our contribution is valuable and valued. Yes, everyone.

YOUR ASSIGNMENT: Make a list of the things you appreciate most about yourself. Notice any comments that would limit or belittle the items you choose. Complete your Daily Evening Review.

DAY 23

If we were to listen only to the grousing of egocentric karmic conditioning, we would be convinced that life consists of problems, lacks and deprivations, failures, and future calamities to stress over and attempt to avoid.

YOUR ASSIGNMENT: Make a list of the things you are grateful for about yourself and your life. Again, watch for voices that want to comment on your choices for the list. Complete your Daily Evening Review.

DAY 24

There are many spiritual types who have reported that their primary spiritual or religious practice has been "thank you." Just that. A simple "thank you" repeated throughout the day.

YOUR ASSIGNMENT: Say "thank you" either silently or aloud (aloud is better!) each time you can remember today. (To aid your memory, this would be a good day for the string-around-your-finger, watch-on-the-other-wrist technique.) When you wake up (perhaps hang a reminder from the ceiling), with your breakfast, as you brush your teeth (perhaps looking yourself in the eyes as you say it), when the car starts, when you see something you find beautiful, when you think of a loved one, when someone is kind, when something goes well, when you find yourself present for no reason, when you remember to approach something as an opportunity rather than a problem, when you get to choose something just because it's what you want... The moments for "thank you" are endless. Complete your Daily Evening Review.

DAY 25

One of my favorite sayings is "Willingness is what's there when 'I' doesn't want to." We're not always identified with a part of our self who <u>wants</u> to. That's not a problem as long as we're <u>willing</u>. I may not want to get up three times in the night with the baby, but I'm willing to. I am willing to because who I really am (conscious, compassionate awareness) is bigger than any little subpersonality who has slipped into the driver's seat of my life at the moment of choice.

YOUR ASSIGNMENT: Flex those willingness muscles by mentoring yourself through a simple task you would usually allow conditioning to turn into drudgery. Complete your Daily Evening Review.

DAY 26

When we're "in love," the pesky, annoying little details of life are not a problem. If the car breaks down, it just means we have extra time together while we wait for the tow truck. If I'm not in love, the broken-down car means a stressful conversation about what I'm late for and how much this is going to cost. The situation is the same except for the "in love" part. Being mentored through life by conscious, compassionate awareness is being "in love."

YOUR ASSIGNMENT: Find a place that is beautiful to you (preferably outside in nature if that's possible). As you are either sitting or walking slowly (slowly enough not to require you to lose touch with your surroundings), recall a time when you felt unconditionally loving. Perhaps you felt this for a parent or grandparent when you were a child, maybe for a sibling, for a best friend, for your own child, or for a pet. The object is irrelevant; the feeling is what's important. Practice returning to that feeling several times during the day, especially before going to sleep. Complete your Daily Evening Review.

DAY 27

We're nearing the end of this retreat. There is much cause for celebration! (Notice if anyone has anything to say about that.)

YOUR ASSIGNMENT: Decide how you are going to celebrate the completion of the first round of your compassionate self-discipline retreat. Will you celebrate alone? Will you invite a friend or partner? Would you like to have a whole crowd to celebrate with? Will you tell others about your accomplishment? Complete your Daily Evening Review.

DAY 28

You have learned and practiced many things during the past few weeks:
You have been sitting in meditation, practicing coming to the present, to HERE, to the breath, and letting everything else go. You have listened to voices and practiced hearing them without believing them. You have worked with subpersonalities and learned the difference between them and the voices of self-hatred. You have learned that quitting does not mean failure; it means "time to start again." You've questioned conditioned beliefs. You've increased your ability to pay attention. You've worked with conscious, compassionate awareness and mentoring. And, hopefully, you've learned that kindness will take you to places punishment never could.

YOUR ASSIGNMENT: Correct and expand this list to include what you've seen and learned over the past few weeks. Complete your Daily Evening Review.

DAY 29

The components of a happy life: appreciation, gratitude, kindness, willingness, love, and compassionate awareness. Conditioning, self-hatred, worry, the voices, the stories, fear, anxiety, past and future concerns, urgency, loss, lack and deprivation, "something wrong," and "not enough" contribute nothing that will lead to a happy life. Nothing. They are just useless.

YOUR ASSIGNMENT: See which of the above is your greatest challenge to living a happy life. Do you get caught up in stories? Do you worry? Do self-hating voices beat you down into depression, hopelessness, or despair? Does urgency convince you that you don't have time to be HERE, to be kind? Complete your Daily Evening Review.

DAY 30

CONGRATULATIONS! Let the celebrations begin!

YOUR ASSIGNMENT: For the rest of your life:

1) Do something kind for yourself every day.
2) Say something loving to yourself every day.
3) Do something that is just for you each day.
4) Think of something you've always wanted to do (preferably impractical and/or frivolous) and do that.
5) Make up your own version of items 1 to 4 and do that every day or as often as you choose.
6) Complete your Daily Evening Review.*

*Come up with your next commitment and begin again at Day 1.